The Fabian Society

The Fabian Society has played a central role for more than a century in the development of political ideas and public policy on the left of centre. Analysing the key challenges facing the UK and the rest of the industrialised world in a changing society and global economy, the Society's programme aims to explore the political ideas and the policy reforms which will define progressive politics in the new century.

The Society is unique among think tanks in being a democratically-constituted membership organisation. It is affiliated to the Labour Party but is editorially and organisationally independent. Through its publications, seminars and conferences, the Society provides an arena for open-minded public debate.

GW00381547

i

Fabian Society
11 Dartmouth Street
London SW1H 9BN
www.fabian-society.org.uk

 Fabian ideas
Series editor: Ellie Levenson

First published December 2003

ISBN 0 7163 0609 3
ISSN 1469 0136

British Library Cataloguing in Publication data.
A catalogue record for this book is available from the British Library.

Printed by Crowes complete print, Norwich

Contents

About the author

Gisela Stuart has been Labour MP for Birmingham Edgbaston since 1997. She was one of two House of Commons' representatives on the European Convention and a member of the Presidium of the Convention on the Future of Europe. Gisela is a member of the House of Commons Foreign Affairs Select Committee.

1| Introduction

The European Union has been successful in binding together countries that spent the last centuries fighting wars with each other. Together with NATO, it has helped to ensure peace and prosperity. From 2004 it will embrace countries that have always been European in their heritage, but that had been locked out behind the iron curtain. The European Union is now making the most significant decisions about its future structure since the Treaty of Rome first established the European Community in 1957.

As a modern European – German by birth and British by choice – I am a first hand beneficiary of Europe's freedoms. A whole generation of people now travel and work across Europe, largely taking for granted the benefits they are reaping from the 'four freedoms' which formed the basis of the European Community back in 1957 – freedom of movement of goods, freedom of movement of persons, freedom to provide services and freedom of movement of capital

These opportunities changed my life. When I came to the UK in 1974, I did not need a work permit, had the right of residence and could go on to a British university. Now after 30 years in this country, I have not only succeeded in learning English, which was the original purpose of my visit to Britain, but am now the

1

democratically elected Member of Parliament for Birmingham Edgbaston. In 1939, the constituency was represented by Neville Chamberlain. Now it is represented by a woman born near Munich. To my children the mere notion of Germany and Britain going to war against each other would seem sheer fantasy.

No one needs to convince me that European cooperation has been a force for good. That is why I want to make sure that there is a European Union which is effective and democratic – and which is able to evolve so as to achieve the needs and aspirations of its peoples. I do not want us to become complacent as we seek to shape a new Europe. And that is why I believe that we need a better and more informed debate about Europe in Parliament and beyond.

A Constitution for Europe

The Convention on the Future of Europe brought together politicians from 28 countries over a period of sixteen months. The result was a Draft Treaty establishing a Constitution for Europe. The document is now being finalised by heads of government in an Intergovernmental Conference which was inaugurated at the Rome Summit in early October 2003. I served as one of two House of Commons representatives on the Convention and as a representative of National Parliaments on the Presidium, the small group charged with putting together the draft. (I was the only woman on the Presidium.)

When I was appointed by the House of Commons I entered the Convention with enthusiasm. I did not – and do not – prejudge the outcome of the Intergovernmental Conference. But I confess, after sixteen months at the heart of the process, I am concerned about many aspects of the draft Constitution. The enlarged European Union must be made to work better, but I am not convinced the proposed Constitution, as it stands, will meet the needs of an expanding Europe.

The most frequently cited justifications for a written Constitution for Europe have been the need to make the Treaties more understandable to European voters and the need to streamline the decision-making procedures of the European Union after enlargement. I support both of these aims. But the draft document, in four parts and 335 pages in the official version, is hardly the handy accessible document to be carried around in a coat pocket which some had hoped for at the outset. From my experience at the Convention it is clear that the real reason for the Constitution – and its main impact – is the political deepening of the Union. This objective was brought home to me when I was told on numerous occasions: 'You and the British may not accept this yet, but you will in a few years' time.'

The Convention brought together a self-selected group of the European political elite, many of whom have their eyes on a career at a European level, which is dependent on more and more integration and who see national governments and national parliaments as an obstacle. Not once in the sixteen months I spent on the Convention did representatives question whether deeper integration is what the people of Europe want, whether it serves their best interests or whether it provides the best basis for a sustainable structure for an expanding Union. The debates focused solely on where we could do more at European Union level. None of the existing policies were questioned.

The British problem?

There seems, however, to be a problem with making this case if you are a British pro-European. Our reputation as Europe's 'awkward squad' gets in the way. Traditional British ambivalence towards Europe, with a history of hesitancy about every step towards closer European integration before generally joining in the end, has left Britain accused of being 'reluctant

Europeans'. Jean Monnet, who led the movement to unify Western Europe in the 1950s and 1960s and is often called the father of the European Community, had his own explanation for this, suggesting: 'There is one thing you British will never understand: an idea. And there is one thing you are supremely good at grasping: a hard fact. We will have to make Europe without you – but then you will have to come in and join us.'

However, the British reputation is a little unfair. After all, Britain is the only country to have had an application to join the European Union turned down twice. The fact that Britain did not join until 1973 was not entirely its own fault. That we strove to join, voted to stay in and have remained engaged members of the Union does at least suggest some doggedness in our attitude. And whatever Britain's record for having missed various European buses or trains, as it is often described, nobody can accuse the present government of having been a reluctant participant in the Convention on the Future of Europe. To that extent we have become good Europeans rather than reluctant Europeans. But what does that mean? Being a 'good European' does not mean accepting the status quo or even a consolidation or 'tidying up' of the status quo. Neither does it mean that the European constitution is less important than it is.

Peter Hain, the British Government's representative on the Convention, said that 'three quarters of it [the Constitution] is tidying up'. But that still left a quarter that he admitted on another occasion was 'creating a new constitutional order for a new united Europe'.

In the past most politicians have focused on the economic rather than the political implications of the European Union. The debate about Europe's future is a battle of ideas and ideologies. The European Union has always been a deeply political project.

4

The Intergovernmental Conference and beyond

Convention President Valery Giscard d'Estaing and others have urged governments not to unravel the document. But, as the British Government enters the final stages of the negotiations, we must be clear about what is in both the United Kingdom's and the European Union's long-term interests. These are interdependent. As the Foreign Secretary has himself said: 'A strong Union is made up of strong Member States working within flexible, transparent and accountable decision making procedures.' This pamphlet sets out a constructive agenda for reform which would help enable the European Union to meet these goals.

This Treaty establishing a Constitution brings together all that has been agreed in the past and introduces significant new changes to the EU. It will be difficult to amend and will be subject to interpretation by the European Court of Justice. And if it remains in its current form, the new Constitution will be able to create powers for itself. It cannot be viewed piecemeal; its sum is more than its parts. To assess its implications, we have to look at its underlying spirit.

The Constitution defines not just institutional arrangements, but also the balance of power, values and objectives. This Constitution is unusual in that it also initiates processes for future development with the aim of deeper and ever closer integration. Where integration can be deepened no further, this text has rigid rules as for example in the list of exclusive competences of the Commission. Power at the centre cannot be returned to Member States. Where the political climate means that certain ideas for further integration are not yet acceptable, the Draft Constitution creates the structure for a process to develop later.

This Constitution is the most important political issue facing Europe today. The Government does not have to accept it.

Enlargement will go ahead and the European Union will continue.

Democratic legitimacy is not mysteriously divined by a group of some 200 self-selected people meeting in Brussels. The details are to be thrashed out and negotiated over by governments at the Intergovernmental Conference. But this is not just a matter for governments. It is also a matter for parliaments and people. We need to make sure that the people agree with the direction their political leaders are taking them.

So far the British Government has resisted the call for a referendum but is likely to come under further pressure on this issue. The final judgement will, in part, depend on the precise text. And there will be those who argue that a referendum is inappropriate for the complex issues involved in the Constitution. On the other hand, general elections deal with a bundle of complex issues. There is a problem in the sense that a European Constitution played no part in Labour's Manifesto at the last election and in theory one option might be to give Members of Parliament a free vote in the House of Commons, but there are clearly problems with this too. Some people have suggested that the 2004 European elections might be the time for the British electorate to give their view on the European Constitution, but in practice we know these elections are generally fought on domestic issues.

But one way or another the contents of the Constitution must be given proper democratic scrutiny and debate. I think that the Government will face increased pressure to allow MPs a free vote if they continue to rule out a referendum. Without this process of democratic scrutiny there will be a strengthening in the tide of euro scepticism, not just in Britain but in other countries too. The recent vote in Sweden was not just against the euro. It was a vote against a political establishment that was taking people along a route to they knew not where, but did not like.

But scrutinising Europe democratically will also mean changing the way we deal with Europe in Britain too. We have to ensure that Europe's institutions are fit for the task they face – but we should also acknowledge that our own national institutions will need to change if they are to play their part. Westminster and Whitehall must take Europe more seriously and stop seeing it simply as an aspect of our foreign policy but as something at the heart of domestic politics too.

2 | The Politics of Europe

The Labour Government has engaged fully in Europe. Our Ministers and MPs have established closer links with their counterparts. Yet opinion polls continue to show a mixture of ignorance and hostility towards European politics. We politicians can't just assume that this is the electorate's fault; we must have been doing something wrong too. Perhaps we politicians need to start the debate on Europe again, and this time we have to have a debate that openly acknowledges the political nature of the Union.

The changes to the structure of the European Union have come in incremental steps. For many, economic co-operation and the single market were a means to achieve deeper political integration, rather than an end. Politicians who have pushed the project forward have relied on this gradualism and an understandable reluctance among European electorates to get to grips with the complexity of the European Union. This has meant that significant developments have taken place without voters really being aware of them.

Labour and the Constitution

All previous British governments have opposed the notion of a written constitution for Europe. A change was indicated in an article by Foreign Secretary Jack Straw published in *The Economist* in October 2002, outlining his ideas of what a future constitution should look like. The significance of this change was underlined by Valery Giscard d'Estaing's remarks to me in a private lunch when he said 'this was the most significant political event since the summer'.

In many ways the article also reflects Tony Blair's commitment to Europe. He is probably more committed to 'Europe' than any previous Labour Prime Minister and, with the exception of Edward Heath, probably more than any Prime Minister of either party since the Treaty of Rome. While the British Government was initially sceptical about the idea of a constitution for Europe, Tony Blair was in no doubt about the significance of the European Convention and ensured Britain was an active partici-pant from the start. At one stage the French even complained that the British had too much influence.

This was a bit over the top, but the Convention and the Intergovernmental Conference are important because this is the first time that a Labour Government has had the chance to put its imprint on a new European venture before it has been set. Although the Wilson Government made some changes to 'the terms' of British entry before the 1975 referendum, entry into the European Community was negotiated by the Conservatives. While Jim Callaghan agreed to direct elections to the European Parliament in 1979, the most important changes in Britain's rela-tionship with other members of the European Union have come under Conservative Governments, in particular the Single European Act (1986) and the Maastricht Treaty (1992) as well as entry and exit from the Exchange Rate Mechanism (ERM).

What was handed over to the heads of government in summer 2003 was described by the European Convention as 'a draft Treaty establishing a Constitution for Europe'. The British Government's White Paper presented to Parliament talked about 'a draft Constitutional Treaty for the European Union'. The Foreign Office described this change of language as 'our own shorthand'. But it is precisely this kind of change of language which makes people distrust anything to do with the European Union. The language is either vague or obscure and it's difficult to work out what words really mean. Some lawyers will argue that it does not matter whether we call this a treaty or a constitution because as far back as 1986 the EEC Treaty was described by the courts as the Community's 'basic constitutional charter'. But it matters to people; signing treaties is something done by nation states, while constitutions are associated with the rules of a state.

The British Government must spell out the consequences of accepting the Constitution. If after this treaty establishing the Constitution there will be no further treaties, then this will need to be made clear and justified. We must step back – without jumping to any conclusion on whether the idea of a constitution is good or bad – and look at the kind of European Union we would have if this is ratified. We have to give the answers to some basic questions in language that people can understand. What is the Union for? What powers should be exercised collectively and what should remain with Member States? Why shouldn't some powers be returned to Member States? Where is qualified majority voting appropriate and where is unanimity essential? How do we ensure democratic accountability for decisions?

As party politicians we must come out of our boxes. Conservatives are too afraid to support anything good about Europe and many in the Labour Party are too reluctant to oppose some of the nonsense. And both for the same reasons: the issue of Europe has become tribal. Those in favour argue that European integration is good, without being specific. Those who find fault are able to illustrate specific shortcomings, but fail to offer a real alternative. The antis win the battles, whilst the pros win the war. This is suffocating a proper debate on what is really at stake.

This is an extremely important moment for the future development of Europe. The framework that was designed for 'the Six' – the original members of the Community – has come under increasing strain as membership expanded. The next enlargement brings in more new countries than in any previous expansion. The world has changed too. Opposition to the Soviet threat no longer serves as a source of European identity, and the post-war economic conditions that sustained the European social model have gone too. Europe has to change, but the process risks setting 'core' against 'periphery', big countries against small countries and those who see Europe through the eyes of the long-dominant Christian Democratic tradition and those that see it extending to Turkey and beyond.

Politicians have not been very good at explaining what the European Union does. The public and the media only tend to take notice when something happens that they don't like. On reflection most people may well decide that they are content with the Union. But they need to be clear about the political direction in which it is going if the draft Constitution is accepted. This is not about leaving the European Union or staying in the European Union; it is about making sure we create a political structure for Europe which serves the people.

Europe in Britain

A reform agenda for greater democratic engagement with Europe also needs to change the way that Britain deals with Europe. Few MPs and opinion formers can competently deal with EU issues. Central and basic parts of the European process – even that the European Commission has the sole right to initiate European laws, for example – seem to remain a mystery to many. Those that do know about the detail – Euro-enthusiasts

11

and Euro-sceptics alike – are often treated with suspicion by their colleagues. Having been immersed in the detail of European issues throughout the Convention, I can understand why.

Responding to public concerns abut the direction of the European project by saying 'don't be silly, nothing like this is going to happen' or 'it's going to happen anyway, so don't try to stop it' just won't do. Europe and its impact on British politics and society are too important to go on like this. We cannot simply make Europe more transparent and democratic 'over there' – vital though this is. We also need to think about how the European Union connects with our domestic political system. Thirty years into our membership, over half of our domestic laws originate in Europe. We need to stop seeing Europe as part of our foreign policy debate and start to integrate it seriously into our national politics. If we are to demand equality with European institutions for our national parliaments and if we are to argue for the principle of subsidiarity to be taken seriously, then we must make sure that our domestic political architecture is up to the job.

Negotiations in Brussels tend to be technically complicated and drag on for a very long time. It is a process that lends itself to lobbying by single interest groups, but makes democratic accountability difficult. Ministers and the House of Commons only get involved at the very late stages, when the vast majority of decisions have already been taken. If we don't enable our own elected representatives to take on a more strategic role in shaping the direction of Europe, we simply hand over power to un-elected civil servants – because they have the factual information at hand, and they have the collective memory which few ministers and MPs have.

Political decisions made at European level have to be anchored in national institutions. At the beginning of every session we devote a whole week to debating the government's forthcoming legislative programme contained in the Queen's Speech. We must start to do the same with the European Commission's Annual Programme. We can do this at the same time as the European Parliament and I see no reason why we should not ask a Commissioner to come to Parliament to answer questions.

It is curious that we treat the European Union as part of the Foreign Office. True there are, and will continue to be, dimensions of our bilateral relations with other Member States which should be handled by the Foreign Office. But the role of Europe Minister needs to be reviewed. The job should be to co-ordinate the 50 per cent of domestic legislation which originates in Brussels across government. So much of it cuts across traditional departmental responsibilities; this makes for poor scrutiny and bad laws. We need to have a regular 'European Questions' slot in the House, just as we have questions to the Prime Minister or the Chancellor of the Exchequer. One option would be the creation of a new Cabinet post of Secretary of State for Europe – located in the Cabinet Office. This single minister would take responsibility for co-ordinating our policies domestic at European level, reporting directly to the Prime Minister and Cabinet and answersing questions in the House of Commons.

The Constitution envisages a stronger role for national parliaments to police subsidiarity. This will only work if we develop better networks with colleagues from socialist parties across Europe. We can also do more to work with our British MEPs at Westminster. They should have access to all the facilities and in specialist committees they should have the right to participate in our proceedings.

British voters will only have confidence in legislation originating from Brussels if they can see that the decision-making process is firmly anchored in the national institutions.

3 | Inside the Convention

Valery Giscard d'Estaing was among those who compared the Convention with the US Constitutional Convention at Philadelphia in 1787. I have to say (with apologies to WC Fields), that I'd rather have been in Philadelphia. It is true that some of the questions addressed by the two conventions might look similar: the power of central government, the balance between small and big states, the union's external representation and its defence, and what happens if a state refuses to ratify the Constitution. But while Philadelphia had the clear purpose of creating a United States, the Convention's objectives were more opaque and the motives of some of its participants were not ones that I share.

Not that this prevented some grandiloquent language when it was launched at the EU Summit at Laeken in 2001. 'Citizens are calling for a clear, open, effective, democratically controlled Community approach, developing a Europe which points the way ahead for the world,' it said. 'The Union stands at a cross-road, a defining moment in its existence. The unification of Europe is near.' This was heady stuff, but there were in fact several very different rationales for the Convention. The existing treaties needed sorting out and the European Union needed to accommodate an expanded and expanding membership. That much was out in the open. But there were other agendas too and at the top was further integration that took a much higher priority than making the European Union democratically accountable. Other objectives included the desire of 'the Six', particularly France and Germany, to retain their effective control in any new structure, linked with a vision of that Europe would challenge the primacy of the US in the wider world. Only some of this was hinted at in the Laeken Declaration which charged the Convention with the task of bringing all the separate treaties into a single legal text, with bringing the European Union 'closer to its citizens', making its institutions more accountable and in line with the needs of its expanded membership and outlining its 'power' in the world.

The European Union has become a complex legal institution that has developed over 50 years with a number of treaties stretching from Rome to Nice. These needed to be brought together to codify the overlapping and impenetrable previous texts. The EU has become very confusing to everyone except the cognoscenti and those based in Brussels and there is a need to clearly define who is competent to do what and how these decisions are to be made. It does not necessarily follow that this requires a Constitution.

Nor is a Constitution necessary to meet another worthwhile objective. It is desirable to streamline the structures with the admission of more members; but enlargement does not depend on the Constitution. Enlargement will go ahead whether the recommendations are accepted or not. The Union's structure will only need revising when we move beyond 25 Member States. This will be the case when Romania and Bulgaria are ready to join, which may be by 2007. There is time to think about the course set out in the Constitution for the European Union. Nonetheless, arguments that 'you can't do what was possible with six members once there are 25' carried the day for moving from unanimity (maintaining national vetoes) to qualified majority voting (in which the majority can impose its will on the minority). This is a bureaucratic justification for making deeply political decisions.

In all the proceedings of the Presidium, there was an unspoken assumption that the *acquis communautaire* – i.e. everything that had been given to the Union as a power or competence – was untouchable. The debates focused solely on where we could do more at European Union level. Any representative who took issue with the fundamental goal of deeper integration was side-lined. Government representatives were accused of being obstructive because they protected national interests. And yet, the concerted efforts by the Commission and the European Parliament to enhance their influence were not seen as power grabbing, but as being good Europeans.

When the new powers for the European Parliament were discussed, I was surprised that there were no demands for giving the Parliament power to censure individual commissioners or to initiate legislation. I was told that the European Parliament was not yet ready for this. Curiously, it was ready to have more power but not more responsibility. There was no discussion about what should remain at national level, only a debate about what could be moved towards the centre.

Underneath everything else was 'the vision thing'. The Prime Minister said in October 2000 in Warsaw that Britain's conception of Europe is rather similar to that of Charles de Gaulle. I doubt that. General de Gaulle said: 'What is the purpose of Europe? It should be to allow us to escape the domination of the Americans and the Russians. The six of us ought to be able to do just as well as either of the superpowers … Europe is a means for France to regain the stature she has lacked since Waterloo, as the first among the world's nations.'

Anti-Americanism remains one of the less edifying driving forces in the process of European integration. Whether it was Valery Giscard d'Estaing telling one of the representatives of the accession countries in the Presidium that his vote did not matter, or Jacques Chirac, the current French President, telling those accession countries who supported the UK and the US over Iraq to behave like well brought up children who are seen but not heard, some things simply have not changed.

Self-appointed elite

Valerie Giscard d'Estaing was appointed as President of the Convention, together with the former Italian Prime Minister Giuliano Amato and the former Belgian Prime Minister Jean-Luc Dehaene as his Vice Presidents. The current fifteen Member States and thirteen other countries which had formally applied to become members of the European Union were asked to nominate one government representative and two representatives from their national parliaments. The European Parliament sent sixteen representatives and the Commission was represented by two Commissioners. A number of organisations had observer status, and every full member of the Convention also had a nominated 'alternate'.

The proceedings were by guided by a Presidium consisting of thirteen Convention members, representing the four institutional groups: governments, the European Parliament, national parliaments and the Commission. It was made up of the President, two Vice Presidents, two European Commissioners, two Members of the European Parliament, three government representatives, two national Parliamentarians (one of whom was me) and a representative from the candidate countries.

The Convention had no formal legal status to make binding decisions on behalf of the institutions represented by its members. The President and Vice Presidents only represented themselves. The Commission pursued its own interests. MEPs spoke for the institution of the European Parliament, not the people who elected them.

Representatives from governments were only accountable in the sense that, eventually, each Member State has to ratify the outcome of the Intergovernmental Conference, to which the conclusions of the Convention were sent. The extent to which national parliamentarians felt obliged to account for decisions at the Convention to their parliaments varied; those from the UK set a good example that was rarely imitated elsewhere.

Those who were directly accountable to their electorate and those who tried to offer alternative visions to what the Union should do and what should be done by Member States were in the minority. During the Convention delegates met in a variety of groupings. I attended the meetings of national parliamentarians, the meeting of all the British representatives which included the British MEPs and the group of European Socialists. We might have been able to find a common view amongst socialist national parliamentarians, but the mechanisms to thrash out ideas were not available. National parliamentarians were numerically the largest group but, in terms of influence, they found it almost impossible to reach common views unless they supported what the European Parliament wanted and in the working of the Convention they were not treated as a discrete constituency. National parliamentarians were the visitors to Brussels, invited to meetings and used to endorse the decisions reached by European interest groups. Several of the national parliamentarians were previous Prime Ministers of their countries; others had been MEPs or were on their national lists for the forthcoming elections. Those who saw their political future in domestic politics were in the minority.

Almost half the members present had no first-hand experience of the workings of the existing Union. They were asked to express a view of how the European Union institutions should be improved, at a time when many of them were still awaiting the final decision about their accession. The representatives from the ten new Member States who had to fight subsequent referenda back home to approve their application were in a particularly difficult position. They could hardly be expected to be too critical. By and large they simply called for 'more Europe', because 'Europe was a good thing'.

The Convention at work

The Presidium was the drafting body, deciding which working groups' recommendations should be accepted almost unchanged (as was the case with the group on the Fundamental Charter of Rights) and which should be almost ignored (such as the one on Social Europe). The President regularly consulted with heads of government to ensure agreement by the large member states, and the Commission and the European Parliament worked closely together, easy for them as they are both based in Brussels.

Laeken had posed a number of specific questions but rather than answering them, after six months of general debates the Presidium presented the Convention members with a skeleton structure of a Constitution. Without debate, it was simply accepted that this was the most appropriate way of fulfilling the Laeken mandate.

The monthly plenary debates were confined to short inspirational speeches with detailed specific discussions reserved for written contributions and the working groups. The Convention had decided early on that it would not take votes, for reasons explained by Valery Giscard d'Estaing: 'They tried this in the previous Convention on the Charter of Fundamental Rights and found it to have been a very bad idea.' Literally thousands of amendments flooded in, and commentators often remarked how difficult it was to see from the outside how decisions were

19

reached on what was deemed to have support and what was discarded.

All I can say is that it was equally difficult from the inside. In the early months, the Presidium members would meet in a small room in the Justus Lipsius Building some fifteen minute walk from the European Parliament. Attendance was limited to the thirteen members, the Secretary General Sir John Kerr, his deputy and the press officer. Sir John Kerr, a former Permanent Secretary of the British Foreign Office, conducted the proceedings inside the Presidium and in the plenary sessions of the Convention with deft diplomatic skill as might be expected from someone who John Major called 'Machiavelli' in his autobiography. The best description of his talents I heard was: 'When Kerr comes up to you and asks for the time, you wonder why me and why now?'

After the first six months, Presidium meetings became more frequent and lengthier. Morning sessions would be followed by private lunches on the top floor. The former Prime Ministers would talk about matters of state, consulting the representative of the Member State currently holding the presidency and sometimes discussing trickier matters. How should we deal with the start of military action in Iraq? Should the President suspend the plenary for an hour in recognition of the seriousness of affairs or should we have a minute of silence. In the end the President chose to wear a black tie.

On several occasions, we would retreat to the Val Duchess – a small palace used by the Belgian foreign minister. It was at one of the dinners at Val Duchess that the skeleton of the draft constitution was given to members of the presidium in sealed brown envelopes the weekend before the public presentation. We were not allowed to take the documents away with us. Just precisely who drafted the skeleton, and when, is still unclear to me, but I gather much of the work was done by Valery Giscard d'Estaing and Sir John Kerr over the summer. There was little time for informed discussion, and even less scope for changes to be made.

In the final weeks, meetings became open ended and some of them lasted into the early hours. Valery Giscard d'Estaing, Giuliano Amato and Jean-Luc Dehaene were an extremely effective trio. Whenever negotiating skills or detailed legal knowledge was needed, the Vice Presidents took over. Giuliano Amato was the man to come up with elegant compromises which were not just the lowest common denominator. Jean-Luc Dehaene was the man to strike deals while Valery Gicard d'Estaing could exert presidential authority when required. But this did not always work

A moment of crisis when the Spanish, backed by two others, blocked the discussions and simply refused to give way was eventually resolved when, while the French Foreign Minister Dominique de Villepin took Valery Giscard d'Estaing out for dinner, the rest of us were able to find a way through the deadlock. There were moments in the sixteen months I spent in close proximity with my fellow Europeans when I had great sympathy with the suggestion of my laptop spellcheck; which, whenever I typed in the word Giscard, replaced it with 'discard'.

The secretariat was very skilful when it came to deciding which decisions of the Presidium would be reflected in subsequent papers. The agenda issued beforehand was simply indicative and the sheer mass of paper which was produced meant that large parts of the text passed through without detailed discussions.

It was only in the final months of the Convention that simultaneous translation was provided for Presidium meetings and we could be accompanied by an assistant to give legal advice. As I was the representative of parliament, not government, I chose to be supported primarily by Speaker's Counsel and Counsel for European Legislation at the House of Commons rather than rely solely on the Foreign Office. It was not unusual for texts to arrive late and only in French. Whenever the President expressed his irritation at my inability to conduct legal negotiations in French, I offered to switch to German. He never took up my suggestion.

Some members of the secretariat showed particular irritation with my insistence that documents be produced in English. On one occasion, a redraft of the articles dealing with defence mysteriously arrived for circulation just before midnight. They were written in French and the authorship was unclear. Verbal reassurances were given to those of us who felt uneasy about approving legal text in an unfamiliar language, that this was little more than a 'linguistically better draft of the earlier English version'. The draft was discarded when some of us spotted that the references to NATO had mysteriously disappeared. Sometimes wordings would be agreed in the Presidium, but these were not always translated into the official texts circulated to the Convention. At other times significant new provisions, such as the so-called 'Passerelle clause' in Article 24 [4], which will be addressed later, would be introduced at a very late stage without much discussion.

The Presidium decided on the timetable and the general conduct of the Convention. Once the broad outline of the Constitutional text had been agreed, working groups were set up to thrash out particular topics in detail. I chaired a group that looked into the role of National Parliaments. The groups which tried to reach a common view on some of the more contentious political issues tended to fail. It was therefore decided not set up a working group on the institutions. This is curious, as institutions are at the heart of any Constitution. I am certain that the institutional settlement proposed will come under the most intense pressure for change in the Intergovernmental Conference.

Consensus. What consensus?

The six founding Member States struck agreements on the Draft Constitution in last-minute deals in the Presidium. From its high-minded beginnings, the Convention became a mixture of individual idiosyncrasies, principled positions and political horse-trading.

Germany ensured that asylum and immigration would not all be decided by Qualified Majority Voting at European Union level, something which the Länder, constituent states, had demanded. The 'Declaration on the Creation of a European External Action Service' was reinstated, despite having been rejected earlier on and, in legal terms, being quite unnecessary. Similarly the provision making it explicit that the President of the Commission could not also hold the post of President of the Council was removed in the last days. Valery Giscard d'Estaing explained this as 'being an unnecessary statement, as both the jobs were so demanding, that one person simply could not combine them'. The truth is that these two amendments reflected the wishes of the German Foreign Minister for the establishment of a European Diplomatic Service and the emergence of a strong single leader of the Union.

At the last minute an article for a 'people's petition' to the Commission appeared as Article 46 (4). It is vaguely worded, opens the door to single pressure groups and, more importantly, undermines national parliaments by giving citizens collectively a right which their elected representatives don't have – the right to ask the Commission to initiate a law. The article appeared because Germany hoped this would help silence the demands in their country for a referendum on the Constitution.

I still cannot recall when the Presidium agreed the provision in the Protocol on the Euro group which says that 'Member States which have adopted the euro shall elect a President for two and a half years'. But I have since been told by a German official that the French not only insisted on the proposal but also on the terminology 'President'. France also retained its ability to go on subsidising their film industry, something they succeeded in portraying as being a very European desire. Meanwhile, Spain's strong objections to the changes in weighting of votes in the Council Ministers were ignored.

Consensus was achieved among those who were deemed to matter and those deemed to matter made it plain that the rest would not be allowed to wreck the fragile agreement struck. The original composition of the Presidium excluded any representatives from the candidate countries but in response to pressure we included what was termed an 'invitee'. According to the strict interpretation of the Laeken mandate, such a person could take part in all the discussions but 'not prevent consensus'. In practice we all forgot about this technical provision, until a very telling moment on the final day. We had lunch together, drank Slovenian wine and accepted as a present a jar of Slovenian honey – all generously provided by the 'invitee'. We went back to discuss whether the French could continue to insist on being able to subsidise the French film industry. As Valery Giscard d'Estaing went round the table asking for individual votes he soon realised that Alojs Peterle, 'the invitee' from Slovenia, had the casting vote. As he said no, Valery Giscard d'Estaing just looked at him and said 'your vote doesn't count'. This provoked a storm of outrage and the President was left in no doubt about what the rest of us thought of this. But I did tell Alojs Peterle: 'If you remember nothing else about the 16 months here, remember this moment. Despite all the friendly chat and food and wine, when it comes to the crunch some people are prepared to turn round and say you don't count'.

But it was not just the accession countries which felt excluded. In the final stages of the Convention, a number of delegates, myself included, made it clear that we could not endorse the text as it stood and that it should be regarded as no more than a basis for further discussions. Neither could we endorse the text on behalf of the parliaments who had sent us. Yet, hardly was the ink dry on the Draft than this was turned into an endorsement by all those present and governments were warned not open up the carefully achieved compromises. The 'consensus' reached was only among those who shared a particular view of what the Constitution was supposed to achieve.

Since the beginning of the Intergovernmental Conference the representatives of the European Parliament have expressed frustration at the post-Convention negotiations. They argue that governments, particularly new entrants, are trying to reopen issues settled in the Convention because they have not understood them. Even more surprising is their argument that the Draft should not be touched because the Convention proceedings 'were legitimate in the view of public opinion'. Where they get this from is a mystery to me. According to Eurobarometer, which conducts opinion surveys across the European Union, the public by and large has no idea what the Convention on the Future of Europe was all about. The figures published in November 2003 suggest – if one accepts the Commission's interpretation – that two thirds of Europeans welcome a European Constitution and more than 80 per cent are in favour of a constitutional referendum. And yet the same survey found that while 62 per cent of Greeks are not aware of the existence of the draft Constitution, some 75 per cent of Greeks want amendments to it. This perhaps encapsulates a wider view of Europe, that whatever is coming out of it, it is bound to need change.

Despite sixteen months of work and thousands of words written and spoken, it is clear that the Constitution is little understood and that the Convention did not succeed in its stated aim of involving the public at large.

4 | What's in the Draft Constitution?

The draft European Union Constitution document is in four parts and runs to 335 pages. It is not exactly a pocket book but it does bring all the various treaties into one comprehensive single document.

Within the scope of a short pamphlet it is not possible to offer a full guide to the Constitution's provisions. But this chapter summarises some of the most important issues at stake while Chapter Five sets out some of the reforms which I would like to see both the British and other governments push for in the Intergovernmental Conference in order to create an effective and democratically legitimate European Union.

A constitutional settlement is fundamentally about the balance of powers between institutions – and this is particularly important within as finely balanced and complex a political system as the European Union, which seeks to combine national democracies with a new form of multilateral cooperation. I will focus on three central issues in the draft European Constitution – the relationship between the Member States and the European institutions; the balance of powers and competences between those institutions themselves; and the question of how the Union should be financed.

Babies or buns?

I was puzzled when former Italian Prime Minister Giuliano Amato urged the Presidium 'to make up our mind whether we wanted to make babies or buns'. I later understood what he meant – buns come out of the oven fully formed, whereas babies grow.

Giuliano Amato's view was that those, like himself, who wanted the European Constitution to continue momentum towards 'ever closer union' in Europe could best pursue this by planting 'organic' provisions which would allow the Constitution to grow and be changed from within without requiring further ratification by member states or their elected national parliaments. He later complained that 'we wanted a girl, but got a boy' – this was his way of expressing his disappointment that the concept of 'organic law' was rejected as going too far. But I am sure he was more than aware that some organic provisions had made their way into the text.

My fundamental objection to them is that assent for changes moves to the European institutions, without the further involvement of Westminster or other national Parliaments. The issue is therefore crucial for those concerned about the balance of power between the Member States and the institutions of the European Union itself.

What is in the draft Constitution: A citizen's guide

Part One: Core Principles of the European Union
This covers the definition of objectives of the Union, fundamental rights and citizenship of the Union, Union competences, the Union's institutions, the exercise of Union competence, the democratic life of the Union, the Union's finance, the Union and its immediate environment and Union membership.

Part Two: The Charter of Fundamental Rights
Comprises the Charter of Fundamental Rights, with chapters headed dignity, freedoms, equality, solidarity, citizens' rights and justice. The Charter was adopted in the Nice Treaty; it is intended to apply to the actions of the European Union and its institutions, rather than have domestic application.

Part Three: The Substantive Policies of the Union
It describes in over 100 pages the European Union substantive policies, as well as detailed institutional, procedural and financial provisions. Areas covered include internal market, economic and monetary policy, policies specific to employment, social policy, social and territorial cohesion, agriculture and fisheries, the environment, consumer protection, transport, the trans-European networks, research and technological development and space as well as energy, and the area of freedom, security and justice. It defines the Union's external action such as common and foreign security policy, common commercial policy, co-operation with other countries and humanitarian aid, international agreements and the implementation of the solidarity clause. It lists those areas where the Union may take action if member states have not done so; these include public health, industry, culture, education, vocational training, youth, sport, civil protection and administrative co-operation.

Part Four: General and Final Provision.
This section includes the symbols of the Union - the flag of twelve golden stars on a blue background, an anthem based on Beethoven's Ode to Joy, the motto 'United in diversity', the euro as its currency and May 9th as 'Europe Day'. It lists the 21 official languages of the Union and describes how the document will be ratified and revised. A number of protocols are attached,

dealing with issues like the role of national parliaments, the principles of subsidiarity and proportionality, the representation of citizens in the European Parliament and the weighting of votes in the European Council and the Council of Ministers, the Euro Group, Amendments to Euratom Treaty [European Atomic Energy Community], as well as a 'declaration on the creation of a European external actions service.'

The most obvious 'organic' provision is Article 24 (4), the Passerelle Clause, which allows the Council of Ministers to move from the national veto to Qualified Majority Voting, subject to governmental, but not necessarily parliamentary, approval, and Article 17, the Flexibility Clause, which gives the Commission wider powers to act where there is no specific treaty basis. This latter provision had existed before, but was limited to 'the operation of the common market', where there was a clear rationale for Commission action to ensure the creation of a single market. Widening the scope of this to the policies defined in Part III – which covers the EU's substantive policies across the board – would allow the Commission on a one-off basis to create its own powers, albeit with some safeguards. This change was simply driven through in the Presidium by presenting to the Convention a text which did not fully reflect what had been agreed.

But at least Article 17 was discussed, and at an early stage. This was not the case for Article 24 [4] – the Passerelle clause. It appeared at a very late stage and only after it became clear that there was considerable opposition to a wholesale extension of qualified majority voting. The first I ever saw of it was late on a Friday afternoon – 5pm on June 6 2003, to be precise. The Presidium had a meeting which started at 3pm and I made it clear that I was happy to stay on till Saturday, but if there was nothing significant on the agenda I would have to leave at

5.20pm to catch the last flight back to Birmingham. Nothing significant was discussed for two hours and at 5.00pm several pages of new text were circulated – just to be approved for release to the Convention. The text contained Article 24[4] – I refused to discuss it in just twenty minutes and insisted that we would do so the following Monday. So I suppose the headline 'British walk-out over Giscard trick' in Saturday's British papers had an element of truth to it, but for once I would not lay the blame for it at Valery Giscard d'Estaing's feet. But as the Article has since been hailed by the European Parliament as a 'great achievement' I assume it was part of some institutional bargaining I had not been privy to.

In contrast, the draft Constitution contains no mechanism to review and return powers from the Union to Member States. I discussed such a clause with German Convention members, some of whom were supportive in principle. They even had a word for it, a *Rückverlagerungsklause*. But there was not sufficient political support for this and we could not agree on areas where such a clause may be applied. This is a serious omission and makes the Union's structure inflexible.

The Constitution as it stands does not change any of the policies of the European Union but it does change the way decisions will be made in future. It is not just a document which sets out rigid rules to determine future actions or how power is to be exercised but it also initiates processes. Predicting its precise impact or assessing its significance is therefore difficult, but the direction is clear: more political and economic integration.

The *acquis communautaire* has been incorporated into the Constitution in its entirety. But in practice the present scope of the *acquis* is not reconcilable with the professed objective of subsidiarity and taking decisions at the lowest feasible level. Competence acquired by the European Union is never returned to Member States. Disputes about subsidiarity only really arise in those areas of competence not yet acquired by the European Union. And the definition of shared competence is a residual one, which means Member States can only act in as far as the Union has not decided to act.

The draft Constitution proposes in at least 36 separate policy areas that the national veto be abolished so that decision-making does not become paralysed in a Union of 25 members. It will remain for sensitive areas such as defence, foreign policy, tax and social security matters. The Constitution no longer allows for new national opt-outs which have been used in the past to protect particular national interests. It is intended that the opt-outs for the single currency for the UK and Denmark remain, as do the special arrangements for the countries who have not agreed to lift border controls under the Schengen agreement.

Rather than particular countries opting out from a policy, the Constitution makes provisions for 'enhanced co-operation' in Article 43 and structured co-operation in Article 40 (6). Enhanced co-operation allows a group of Member States to move ahead in areas where the Union does not have exclusive competence, whilst structured co-operation only applies to areas relating to the implementation of the common foreign and security and defence policy. The latter is potentially divisive as it can be used as a mechanism for the core countries, particularly France, to impose their authority on the enlarged European Union as they did with 'the Six'.

The French Foreign Minister Dominique de Villepin made his views quite clear in his Dimbleby lecture in October 2003 when he spoke about Europe's role in the world and said: 'Together with Germany, our three countries have the political will, the economic significance and the military capabilities than can shape our continent ... we have a duty to posterity: to find the path which will lead to a new world.'

The Maastricht Treaty established a pillar structure. The first pillar referred to the European Community in which power had been conferred by Member States to the European Community and where, in many areas, the European Parliament has the right to be a co-legislator. But the second and third pillars of the European Union made special provision for areas which were deemed to be particularly sensitive to Member States and therefore had special decision making procedures. The areas concerned are justice and home affairs and foreign, defence and security policy. The new Constitution brings all previous treaties into a single text and this largely removes the pillar structure. There are still some special provisions, but the presumption has been reversed in favour of the operation of the general principles of EC law. The policy area most affected is justice and home affairs. European Union policy on refugees and asylum and some aspects of immigration policy will be decided by majority vote. The United Kingdom has fought for a move to Qualified Majority Voting in this area. Asylum and immigration clearly has to be resolved on a Europe-wide basis. It is in our interest to ensure that all countries fulfil their responsibilities. The draft Constitution also provides for the harmonisation of criminal law and sentencing for certain serious crimes with cross-border implications, such as corruption and drug-trafficking.

The Constitution also alters the legal nature of the European Union. Article 6 simply states: 'The Union shall have legal personality.' By merging the European Community and the Treaty of European Union into a single legal personality, the Union will be able to enter into international agreements across the whole range of activities covered by the former three pillars. Some have argued that this has more symbolic than legal significance while others have hailed the creation of a single legal personality as one the Convention's greatest achievements. Others are still concerned about its implications. For example, former European Ombudsman Jacob Söderman now argues for a referendum in Finland on the Constitution on the basis that with a legal personality the European Union has powers beyond national constitutions to make laws that concern all of its citizens.

One of the most important tests of the powers of Member States must surely be their democratic right to decide whether to accept the proposed Constitution. And yet the final page of the draft text states: 'If, two years after the signature of the Treaty establishing the Constitution, four fifths of the Member States have ratified it and one or more Member States have encountered difficulties in proceeding with ratification, the matter will be referred to the European Council.' In this context the word 'difficulties' is an odd one, implying that ratification is the norm and the expected response. A country not ratifying is not behaving normally or rationally and needs in some way to be helped, or more likely pressurised, to the right conclusion. Of course it is said that we can't have one country (or perhaps several) holding things up. But this new Constitution repeals the Treaty of Rome and in that Treaty it is clear that repeal requires unanimity. It is not a matter of a country being difficult – that is what they all signed up to. It is the basis of the European Union.

Europe's institutions and the Constitution

I was surprised that the European Convention spent very little time discussing the powers of the European institutions. After all, the balance of power between institutions is essential to making the system work. The Constitution effectively papers over a number of underlying tensions and different views of what the European Union should do – for example, tensions between national 'representation' and collective European bodies; and tensions between big and small countries in getting the balance right for easier decision-making in an enlarged Union.

There is a danger that the general public will have some difficulty in comprehending this new institutional structure. For example, the Union is destined to have four presidents: a President of the European Parliament, a President of the European Council, a President of the Commission and a President of the Euro Group. The term 'President' is understood in different ways. In some countries it is a figurehead; in others, it is the pinnacle of centralised power.

The Constitution does make some good institutional changes. The European Council will no longer have a presidency which rotates to a different national government every six months, but it will have a new President of the Council who is elected every two and a half years to give greater continuity and coherence to the Union's internal and external policymaking. That the Council of Ministers will now meet publicly when agreeing legislation is a positive step forward for accountability and transparency.

But other issues are more difficult. Decision making rules are at the heart of any political system – but what is the right balance between the large and small Member States? The Constitution's new voting rules mark a considerable shift to the big States. Under current rules, the big six (Germany, France, Britain, Italy, Poland and Spain) can be outvoted by the remaining 19 and Belgium, the Netherlands and Luxembourg together have the same weight as Germany, which has three times their combined populaion. The Constitution proposes a new 'double majority' rule so that EU laws can be passed if half the members, representing at least 60 per cent of the population vote for it. In a Union of 25, the six biggest states account for 74 per cent of the European Union population. With the new proposals, the Commission will have an easier task when seeking consensus in the Council of Ministers because it can find a larger number of combinations which make up the required majority. This makes it easier to get decisions, but it assumes that this is desirable in all policy fields.

Britain is one of the big countries – so this might be thought to benefit us. Some envisage a Franco-German-British triumvirate to 'run' Europe. But this objective reflects a deeply unhistorical perspective of Britain. It is not in Britain's long term interests to construct an EU that is 'run' by anyone as a directorate, even assuming that Germany and France were ready to play this game. In the French case in particular, it is difficult to imagine them doing so for anything more than short-term tactical considerations.

The Constitution proposes a reduction in the size of the Commission. While it is easy to understand why small countries in particular oppose the loss of a European Commissioner from each country, this does demonstrate a tension at the very heart of the system. After all, the Commissioners, like the members of the European Central Bank, are not at all supposed to 'represent' national interests but rather to be objective guardians of a broader European interest. No doubt some observe this more than others but the inconsistency exposes the gap between form and reality.

The Union's own resources

It is impossible, in a short pamphlet, to give a detailed list of all the areas where the draft Constitution potentially legislates for far-reaching changes in European Union decision making and where this shifts the balance of power between the supranational and the intergovernmental. There is a Catch-22 here – the draft is so complex that it is difficult to understand; yet I am convinced that those who come to understand it may be forgiven for thinking that they have gone mad in the process! Nevertheless, I offer one area as illustration, an area which is both controversial and highly relevant to Britain: the Union's resources.

Europe's institutions and the Constitution

The European Commission – Article 25 & 26
The Commission is the European Union's Executive, with many government-like functions including proposing new legislation to the Council and the European Parliament for approval. There are currently 20 Commissioners – one for each country and two for the five largest countries. Commissioners are charged with ensuring the correct application of the Treaties and acting in the European interest without regard to their nationality. The Constitution proposes that every country will have one Commissioner until 2009; after that a two-tier system of voting and non-voting Commissioners will operate, creating an inner core of fifteen Commissioners. This means that each country will have a voting Commissioner for ten years in every fifteen. The Constitution leaves the Commission with the sole right to initiate legislation, giving it a pre-veto over which proposed laws can be discussed. The Commission Presidency will be chosen by governments, by Qualified Majority Voting, but MEPs must approve of the choice.

The European Council – Article 20 & 21
Heads of Government meet regularly and every six months the presidency moves to another country. Their meetings are referred to as European Summits. The Constitution proposes an end to the much criticised rotating Presidency – where each country chairs the European Union for six months – and creates a new position, a full time Chair of the European Council, who will serve for a minimum period of two and a half years, to bring greater coherence and consistency to the European Union's actions.

The Council of Ministers – Article 22 & 23

The relevant Ministers from Member States meet behind closed doors to make decisions about legislation. Most of the negotiations are done by the Committee of Permanent Representatives (COREPER) before ministers make decisions; the United Kingdom's Ambassador to the European Union has considerable influence. Votes are rare, but are taken according to a complex weighted formula called Qualified Majority Voting. In future the Council will meet in public when it makes laws and the voting weights will be changed to give a better reflection of the population of a country. The formula for Qualified Majority Voting is based on 'double majority', a majority of countries and people. This gives large countries more say and makes it easier for the Commission to get agreement.

Foreign Minister – Article 27

This is a new position charged with conducting the European Union's common foreign and security policy. This brings together the roles of the current European Union High Representative and the Commissioner for External Relations. The Constitution is still muddled about where final accountability rests; the Council or the Commission.

European Parliament – Article 19

The 626 members of the European Parliament will grow to 732 after enlargement. MEPs scrutinise the activities of the Commission and have extensive powers over legislation and budgetary procedure. The European Parliament will get more power to influence and reject legislation; the areas where it has the power to co-legislate increase from 34 to 70. It will have the final say on the Union's budget [100 billion euros in 2003] and will be able to amend agriculture expenditure and veto on the Commission's seven-year spending programme.

> **Euro-group [Protocol attached to Treaty]**
> A new protocol allows for ministers of Member States who have adopted the euro to meet as the euro-group to develop ever-closer coordination of economic policies with the euro area. The group will elect a president to serve for two and half years.
>
> **European External Action Service [Declaration attached to Treaty]**
> The Convention called for the creation of this service to assist the future Union Minister for Foreign Affairs, to perform his or her duties. It will be composed of officials from staff from the Council of Ministers and of the Commission as well as staff seconded from national diplomatic services.

The question of how the Union is funded is of supreme political importance, particularly for those who are seeking to build a new, more cohesive political settlement in Europe. As Valery Giscard d'Estaing said to me at a very frosty meeting on the subject, pointing his finger at me while he said it: 'Madame Stuart, people like you and the British will have to realise that the Union cannot survive without an independent stream of income.'

This is an issue to which the European Commission is giving much thought. It has committed itself to undertaking a general review of the operation of its own resources system before January 1 2006. The wording in the draft Constitution needs close inspection.

Article 269 EC currently requires unanimity for the 'system of own resources'. A new Article 53 [3] states: 'A European law of the Council of Ministers shall lay down the limit of the Union's resources and may establish new categories of resources or abolish an existing category. That law shall not enter into force until it is approved by the Member States in accordance with their respective constitutional requirements. The Council of Ministers shall act unanimously after consulting the European Parliament.'

This clause covers the overall limits of the Union's resources and unanimity is applied. However the clause does not mention the level of contribution which an individual Member State may have to make.

That thorny issue appears to be covered in Article 53 [4] which says: 'A European law of the Council shall lay down the modalities relating to the Union's resources. The Council of Ministers shall act after obtaining the consent of the European Parliament.' A European law – unless qualified, which it is not in this clause – only requires Qualified Majority Voting, and lawyers tell me that the word 'modality' could be interpreted to mean the amounts which each country individually contributes.

I raised this issue with Ministers. The response was: 'Would any of the other Member States seriously be thinking of handing Brussels a 'system which would allow a committee in Brussels to extract more and more money from Member States?' I do not know the answer to that question but I, and the British Government, need to urgently clarify this point. If 'modalities' indeed is relevant to how much each Member State contributes to the whole and modalities are subject to Qualified Majority Voting, then it is important. It could mean that exactly such a system is being contemplated in which Britain would lose its veto over its budget contribution and the power to maintain its current rebate.

The authoritative German weekly, *Der Spiegel*, certainly thought that the British had missed a trick. In an article headlined 'Der Schatz im Dschungel' (A Treasure Trove in the Jungle), it expressed the view that the British have overlooked the little fact that their rebate was no longer protected by unanimity.

I had a meeting with the Budget Commissioner Michaele Schreyer on this subject. She told me that the Union needs an independent stream of revenue and it is impossible to have 25 countries voting through their own resources. She suggested a dedicated tax, which would go automatically to the European Union. I told her that I would be happy to consider such a tax, provided it was shown on people's pay slips: Gross Pay, National Insurance Contribution, Income Tax, European Union Tax, and Net Pay. She thought this was a joke in rather bad taste.

What she did not appreciate was the importance of the vote in Parliament on the Union's resources. It would be dangerous to remove this. Even during the darkest days of euroscepticism in Britain, there had never been any political divisions about the Union's financing, because Parliament had a say and voted to approve it. However, MPs would quite rightly object to not being asked.

5| The Europe we need

The Intergovernmental Conference must not merely be a rubber-stamping exercise, upholding fragile compromises reached by the Convention. With nothing less than a new Treaty of Rome being finalised, there is a workable agenda for the British Government in the negotiations ahead. We have to play our part in producing a structure that allows the Union to expand and succeed and, over time, command popular support. It is beyond the scope of a short pamphlet like this to go through a long list of articles in the Constitution where the Government should negotiate changes – after all, the Government itself tabled over 1000 amendments to the Draft during the Convention.

Often it is little words which matter or how, for example, an article in one part relates to a supplementary provision in another, one or other of which may be renegotiated in the Intergovernmental Conference. For example, the Government will have to be very careful that Article IV-2 in the General and Final Provisions, which repeals earlier Treaties and all the Protocols, does not 'accidentally' remove our opt-out on European Monetary Union.

But these detailed changes need to be combined with a strong political vision of the ideas which should inform the European agenda. There is too much muddled thinking in some of the

Constitution. If the final stages of the Intergovernmental Conference become a forum for shabby deals negotiated in the early hours of the morning where jobs in the Commission and locations for agencies are traded in for vital changes in the text then this will discredit the European Union at exactly the time when it is most in the media and political spotlight. This chapter sets out four principles which I believe should underpin a more effective and enlarged European Union.

1. Making the right decisions at the right level

Not enough attention is paid to the question of which decisions should be made where – how we apply the principles of subsidiarity and proportionality and how we work out the type of European legislation we need and the right balance of power between the European institutions. At the moment, there is too often an assumption that everything is best undertaken at European Union level unless a Member State can prove it otherwise.

At the beginning of the Convention, Valery Giscard d'Estaing proclaimed with confidence that no part of the *acquis communautaire* should be regarded as untouchable. I was delighted to hear him say that. He was right – there should be no holy cows. We had the chance to assess whether some of the decisions of the past, even if right for their time, were still appropriate in a different world. Unfortunately the Convention focused only on what more could be done at European Union level, rather than looking again from first principles to see what is best achieved at national or even sub-national level.

We could have had the kind of debate we had here in the United Kingdom when we devolved power to Scotland and Wales. We made some big decisions, like taking matters relating to health away from Westminster and giving them to Edinburgh and Cardiff. This has not led to the break up of the United

Kingdom just as returning powers to Member States would not break up the European Union. Quite the contrary, this flexibility would make the Union stronger and more effective.

It is a major shortcoming of the Constitution that it does not provide for a review mechanism of the exercise and allocation of competences. There are a number of ways this could be put right. The Council of Ministers could be given the right to initiate such a process. If, for example, one third of Member States think that there is an area where we have done as much at European level as is appropriate, the Commission should have to put forward a proposal to facilitate a return of the competence. Alternatively, a committee composed of national parliamentarians from all Member States could review past legislation. Whatever the precise mechanism, the Constitution must allow for a two-way flow of power if we are to take the principle of subsidiarity and proportionality seriously rather than merely paying it lip-service.

The Commission's sole right of initiative for European legislation must also be rethought. The noble idea of the Commissioners as the guardians of the European Treaty, acting only in the best interests of the Union and not taking instructions from their country of origin, was right and necessary 50 years ago when there were only six Commissioners. But now there are twenty and might soon be twenty-five, and with each Commissioner seeking to make their political mark, the Commission cannot be relied upon as the sole guardian of subsidiarity. Indeed, Frits Bolkestein, the European Commissioner for Internal Markets, wrote arguing for stronger safeguards in the Constitution against his own institution's 'tendency to over-regulate'.

The type of Commission action needed to create a Customs Union and a Single Market is rather different from the type of policy-making aimed at creating a flexible, technology-based European economy. That is why in 2001 the Heads of

Government initiated what has become known as the Lisbon Process, to move away from having more European Union-wide laws and inflexible regulations and to instead introduce regular and vigorous peer reviews and sharing of best practice which could lead to national reforms which are tailored to fit circumstances in individual Member States. Yet the Lisbon Process has stalled – and largely because the European Commission had very little interest in what is referred to as 'the open method of co-ordination', not least because it would set limits to the process of integration and check the erosion of the nation state.

In the past the British Government has questioned the flood of European directives and the expansion of Commission competences. Having championed the Lisbon Process approach and the open method of co-ordination, the British Government must insist that the Intergovernmental Conference includes a better method of policy co-ordination in the Constitution so that Europe does not over-regulate, where benchmarking and peer review would be more effective by far.

One potential mechanism which could be built upon is the new right given to national parliaments to review Commission proposals for compliance with the principle of subsidiarity. The so called 'early warning mechanism' does not apply to areas where the Commission has exclusive competence and it cannot look at proportionality – the principle that measures must be necessary to achieve the stated aim. Strengthening this mechanism by extending its remit and giving it the power to make the Commission withdraw a proposal would be a step in the right direction.

One of the most contentious issues at the Intergovernmental Conference will be that of where Qualified Majority Voting should apply and where unanimity and national vetoes should remain. There is an argument to be made for extending qualified majority decision-making to all aspects of the Constitution on the basis that unanimity was possible with six member states but will not be with 25 or more. Yet there are policy areas where maintaining the national veto is essential for the implementation of domestic policy, i.e. those where answers can only be found on the national, rather than the pan-European level. The same applies to those areas where what we need is a common political will which can only be found at head of government level, which is the case with foreign and defence policy.

How the Constitution can be changed – and the need for national parliaments to ratify constitutional amendments – is a vital issue. Just as any new treaty has to be ratified by every single Member State, so do future changes to the Constitution. Any move away from that principle would fundamentally change the nature of the European Union. Article 24 [4] allows for the move from unanimity to Qualified Majority Voting, without requiring the approval of Parliaments, and is in my view unacceptable. Also unacceptable would be any change to the principle of 'conferral' – which means the Union only has those powers specifically given to it by Member States.

The European Parliament is pressing for a system where future changes to the Constitution could be agreed by Heads of Government in the European Council, the Commission and the European Parliament with national parliaments simply being informed of these chanegs. This is a step too far, as are moves to make a distinction between different parts of the Constitution and how they can be changed. At the very end of the Convention, proposals were re-introduced to apply a softer amendment procedure to areas which are deemed as non-constitutional. What is and is not constitutional would be determined by the European Court of Justice which would exclude national parliaments from the process. In my view all the parts of the document must continue to be of equal status.

One argument for ending national vetoes is that countries can always leave if they don't like it. For the first time the Constitution provides for an explicit exit clause. This must not be turned into an expulsion clause. The reasoning that any country which does not approve this Constitution has de facto left the Union is simply not true, even though there were many in the Convention who argued for exactly such an interpretation. A country which does not ratify this Constitution remains party to the existing Treaty on European Union, as do all the other Member States in their relations with that country.

2. The right institutions doing the right thing

The European Union has always been a unique, hybrid political system, combining intergovernmentalism, where Member States reach agreements among themselves, and the community method, where decisions are made by the Commission and European Parliament. The cornerstone of the US Constitution written at the Philadelphia Convention was the separation of powers between the Executive and the Legislature which has been an enduring source of stability in the American political system. The European Constitution should also enshrine a separation of powers – or competences – in the language of the Union.

Over the years the balance has shifted towards the European institutions, not least since we have had a directly elected European Parliament. Although the Constitution lays down the current allocation of competences, whether exclusive or shared, the 'organic' features of the draft that I have described earlier give ample ground for these competences to shift in future. Our Government negotiators need to spot and deal with these unpredictable parts of the constitutional draft.

There are some areas where consensus can only be achieved at Head of Government level. That is why Britain supported giving the Council a more strategic role and argued for the creation of the new post of President of the European Council. Holding office for two and a half years, the Council President will bring strategic direction and continuity to the institution which represents Member States. But the Convention was wrong not to rule out the possibility of the Presidency of the Commission and the Presidency of the European Council being held by the same person.

As Foreign Secretary Jack Straw told the House of Commons on October 20 2003: 'It is extremely important that the two functions are separate, as they reflect the balance of power between the European Council and the European Commission. That separation and balance is one of the reasons why the European Union has been as successful as it has been.'

The final text must make it clear that the same person can not hold both posts. Valery Giscard d'Estaing told the Convention that this was 'unnecessary' – and that the two jobs were simply too big to be done by one person. But such an assurance does not adequately deal with suspicions as to why the wording was removed late in the process.

Nor does the Constitution create clear enough lines of responsibility for the new post of a Foreign Minister for Europe. The proposed structure is in practice unworkable and politically undesirable. Accountability has to be explicit and be firmly anchored in the Council rather than the Commission.

There is a proper role for European countries to cooperate in foreign affairs and defence and hopefully come up with common views. But I hope the Government will not accept the rules for what is described as 'structured cooperation' in Article 40 [6]. This would create a kind of closed-shop for a small core who could go ahead without having to allow other countries to participate at a later stage if they wished to do so.

The decision for the United Kingdom here is a deeply strategic one. By saying yes to structured cooperation, it will signal a fundamental change in our policy. In the past we have never supported the development of a core Europe, indeed we have been seen by many of the smaller countries as a protector of their rights.

As the European Union institutions acquire more powers, we have to be confident that they are 'fit for purpose'. With power come responsibilities. The Constitution suggests a European Commission which is divided into voting and non-voting Commissioners. In theory this should make for a smaller and more efficient decision-making body. This is a good start, but does not go far enough. I regret that the Convention did not stick to the original proposal which would have fixed the total number of Commissioners at fifteen. I hope the British Government will grasp this nettle and insist that we move away from the assumption that every country must have a Commissioner.

A strong Commission which acts in a transparent and accountable fashion is essential, particularly after a decade in which the Commission has not given us much cause for confidence. Its accounts have not been signed off by auditors for nine years in a row. The entire Commission had to resign in 1999 and this year it is engulfed in yet another financial scandal, this time at Eurostat, the European Union's agency for statistics.

But there is little in the Constitution to improve accountability and good governance. The Commission decides what the Council of Ministers can vote on but there are no safeguards to ensure that they only act in the best interest of the Union. It is simply assumed that the Commission is not driven by self-interest. Constitutions are about the exercise and control of power. With so few controls in the text, we have to rely on good-will, and that is not enough. The Constitution should impose a duty of good governance on the Commission President and give individual Commissioners powers to instruct their staff and make them accountable for their actions. For the European

Parliament to be able to hold the executive to account, it should have the power to hold individual Commissioners to account.

The European Parliament will become a co-legislator in many more policy areas. This increase in influence must be combined with greater responsibility to ensure better quality of legislation, including proper impact assessments for legislative proposals. This gives voters a better chance to know who has been responsible for what.

The European Parliament has to be more accountable and efficient if it is to gain greater public confidence. For historic reasons MEPs and their army of translators and support staff shuttle between Strasbourg and Brussels. There is simply no rational justification for this waste of time and money which so angers European taxpayers and which does more than anything else to turn opinion against MEPs who are, in most cases, striving to do a good job. The Convention failed by not insisting that the Constitution establishes Brussels as the sole seat for the European Parliament. This was an unfortunate example of nobody being prepared to pick a fight with the French.

3. Maintaining room for manoeuvre on national policy

Britain is a modern, forward-looking and successful European country with a flexible and competitive economy. If we want to go on being so, we must retain the necessary policy tools such as tax and social security. Trying to entrench a social and economic model that has become outdated and no longer meets the challenges of a global economy is not just bad for Britain; it is also bad for Europe.

Britain's insistence on retaining the national veto on taxation and social security is not a sign that we are being obstructive. Governments are elected on the basis of how much tax they raise and their priorities on how to spend these resources. These are the means by which governments find the right balance appropriate for the needs of their people. There is no such thing as a universal European economic and social model which would be right for all Member States at any given time. That is why these decisions have to stay with Member States.

Let me illustrate this point with one specific example. The Labour Government's working tax credits brought about a fundamental change in the way social security benefits were to be administered, no longer as hand-outs but through the wage packet. It ensured that it was always better to be in work than out of work. It challenged economic assumptions held in many other European countries. We developed a method of dealing with social exclusion and unemployment which has not been copied elsewhere in Europe. It has been a success, but we could not have done it if these matters had been subject to Qualified Majority Voting.

There were many in the Convention who did think the European Union should be able to harmonise levels of taxation, not least the President. The British Government was right when it made tax one of its 'red lines'; it now needs to read the small print of the text very carefully. Article III-62[2] is written in a way which would open a back door into harmonisation. The text refers to matters relating to administrative cooperation in combating tax fraud and tax evasion. Tax fraud is a clear concept; it is illegal. Tax evasion, on the other hand, is differently interpreted in the 25 countries across the Union. The lack of precision in the language could open this area up to a community-wide definition drafted either by the Commission or based on an interpretation by the European Court of Justice. In either case we could end up with tax harmonisation through the back door, without being able to do anything about it.

This scenario is not unrealistic. We have seen such judicial activity in relation to health. Member States have always been

50

clear that health should not be governed by the rules of the internal market. But over the last decade a number of court judgments based on the definition of the 'provision of services' have step by step drawn health into the internal market.

Some might feel that being given the right to go abroad for a hip operation because waiting times in the UK are too long is a good thing. But deciding how much money we spend on health is one of the fundamental building blocks of how we finance the NHS. I for one would not want to see this changed.

The terms used in the Constitution need to be clarified to ensure that tax, social security and the funding of the European Union cannot be interpreted in a way contrary to the politicians' clear intentions.

Laws relating to criminal justice such as admissibility of evidence, definitions of crimes, and levels of sentencing are at the root of citizens' relationship with the State. The Constitution makes some good changes to the way countries can cooperate on cross-border crime and the exchange of information. This is limited to cases involving crimes which are both serious and have a cross-border element. Some had pushed for it to cover crimes which are cross-border or serious, which would have given the European Union far reaching competences. By and large the focus is on mutual recognition of systems rather than attempting harmonisation and this must be right.

However, the Constitution does provide a legal basis for the creation of a European Public Prosecutor. This was an initiative from the Budget Commissioner to deal with fraud against the European Union. This is an example of where the Convention came up with the wrong answer to a real problem. If there is widespread fraud, then this should be dealt with by making the system of awarding and paying subsidies more transparent and accountable. What we need are proper accounting procedures in the Commission and closer co-operation between Member States, not a new institution and another bureaucracy.

Opposition to the inclusion of a treaty base was always countered by the argument that it will not be created unless every country agrees to it. I have never believed in the magic of what is known as the 'unanimity lock'. Either we need a European Public Prosecutor, in which we should set one up, or we don't in which case we leave it out of the text. Putting it into the Constitution in this way is just another example of how ideas for deeper integration never go away but simply go underground. The Government should insist on removing the Treaty base for a European Public Prosecutor.

When it is clear that an objective is best achieved by collective action, power should go to the centre. That is why the United Kingdom has argued for greater use of Qualified Majority Voting on matters dealing with asylum and immigration. When local decision-making is appropriate power should move away from the centre. I would be surprised if many people would argue against fundamental changes to the Common Agricultural Policy. We have to be able to determine where the answer to a particular problem lies and have the scope to be flexible over whether this is at regional, national or European level.

4. Holding our masters to account

Accountability and transparency are at the heart of good government. In 2003 Charter 88 published five democratic tests for Europe which asked about fair representation, means of participation, respect for the rights of individuals, the accountability of institutions and the transparency of decision making. These are important. But for the voter the crucial question is 'can I get rid of them if I don't like what they are doing?' This has always been a problem with the European institutions and the Constitution does not resolve it.

The process of decision making will be more open. Ministers will meet in public when they make laws and there will be a much greater flow of information about Commission proposals. But the public still has no sense of who precisely is responsible for what even though holding decision makers to account is the essence of democracy.

The European Parliament is a co-legislator, together with the Commission and the Council of Ministers. But when people vote in European elections they vote for a domestic political party and not for a government. MEPs have a political relationship with their national governments, but in practice their selection as candidates, and thus their chances for re-election, means that their principle relationship is with their own national political party.

We know how many Labour MEPs there are, but few know how many Socialist MEPs there are let alone whether they vote as a block or according to national interests. The system of regional lists has further added to the alienation – voters no longer have a sense of who their MEP is. Every European election in the UK has been fought by domestic political parties on a largely domestic agenda. The voters have no sense of what policies they support at European level when they cast their vote. They know what a Labour vote means here in Britain – but not what it means in Brussels. The European Parliament works on coalitions across large numbers of political parties and after enlargement there will be 732 MEPs representing anything up to 100 different political parties. It is no wonder that voters are confused and stay at home in droves.

Political parties have to make a choice. We could just accept that fewer and fewer people turn out at European elections because they can't see the point of it. Or we could do more to work towards European political parties, so the ballot paper in Britain would, for example, no longer say Labour but the Party of European Socialists. From my experience in the Convention, we are far from being able to achieve this, even if it were desirable. It would also be possible to make the election of the President of the Commission subject to popular franchise. This would give the voters a real 'outcome' at the end of the election, but it would not solve the problem of remoteness. Alternatively, we could anchor European decision-making in national institutions. We can do this, by giving national parliaments greater powers to police subsidiarity, making Westminster discuss and vote on the planned legislation coming from the Commission and allow our MEPs to take part in our proceedings in Parliament. One way or another, voters have to know where the buck stops.

In my view the only realistic way forward is an anchoring of European decision making in national institutions. In Britain, we still treat Europe as something over there, as if we are not part of it. We are part of Europe and when something is decided in Brussels, it is not something 'done to us by them' but something 'we did with them'. Politicians do little to put this misperception right. Practical proposals to change this are set out in detail in Chapter Two.

6| Conclusion

At the Intergovernmental Conference the Prime Minister has an enormous responsibility. The outcome will either re-establish confidence in the European Union or it will do lasting damage to something I have supported all my life and on every political platform on which I have stood.

My first experience of standing for public office was in the 1994 European Elections. I thought then, and still do now, that it is incumbent on my generation of politicians to do more to explain the benefits of the European Union to an increasingly hostile public. Now, as an MP at Westminster, I realise that we have not done enough to forge closer political links with social democratic parties across Europe. We still have a lot more work to do in the way we work with our fellow MEPs for the benefit of those who have elected us.

The Convention on the Future of Europe was an opportunity to shape Europe for the twenty-first century. Valery Giscard d'Estaing himself made reference to this being the first opportunity to reconsider the future direction of the European Union since the Conference in Messina in 1955. Europe is not just about economics or simply creating a free trade area and a single market within its boundaries, though these are important. The European Union is, and always has been, a political project, even though this has not been something that has been as openly acknowledged as it should have been in Britain.

I want a Europe that reaches beyond the original founding countries and I welcome the current round of enlargement to the East. I hope that before long countries like Romania and Bulgaria, as well as some of Balkan states and Turkey can join. I want a Europe that is inclusive and one that is true to its motto of 'united in diversity'. I also want a Europe that recognises that it has a responsibility to those countries outside the Union. I do not want a fortress Europe, one which only protects its own interests without honouring its wider responsibilities.

It was an enormous honour for me to be one of the House of Commons representatives on the Convention and I approached the task with real enthusiasm. But I am far from convinced that the Convention lived up to the task it had set itself.

The draft Constitution which emerged is based on a political structure that reflects the attitudes which moulded the prevailing political and economic climate of fifty years ago. The world has moved on and the European Union needs to as well if it is to be relevant not just to my generation but to my children's generation.

There is an obvious reluctance to re-open matters that were apparently settled in the Convention, but as I have made clear the process in the Convention was itself riddled with imperfections and moulded by a largely unaccountable political elite, set on a particular outcome from the very start.

The real issue to be addressed is whether this model for Europe is any longer the most suitable. I used to enjoy driving my old Mini, but as it became unroadworthy I knew something else was needed.

There are other models available for Europe too, if Britain and other countries were to choose them, not just the one designed in 1957 and modified from time to time.

These include a European Union with a more overtly federal and democratic structure or alternatively A European Union that has a much less comprehensive political and economic agenda with much of the existing authority of Brussels returned to the democratic accountability of Member States. People will have their own views on the desirability of these and other options, but we should be wary of adopting the phrase coined in another age by another politician : 'There is no alternative'. Influence in Europe has to mean more than that.

There is an understandable desire by those who have served in the Convention to want something lasting to show for their endeavours. Valery Giscard d'Estaing himself wants to secure his place in history, not a dishonourable or uncommon preoccupation among politicians, by giving Europe a written Constitution. On one notable occasion he told us in the Presidium that 'this is what you have to do if you want the people to build statues of you on horseback back in the villages you all come from'.

Many countries will hold a referendum on the Constitution once its final shape emerges. These include countries such as Ireland and Denmark that have long traditions of holding referenda. But there are also countries for which referenda are quite unusual which see this as important enough to justify a vote, including Portugal, Spain, Luxembourg, the Netherlands and the Czech Republic. Even in France there is much support for a referendum.

If this Constitution does not have the support of the people of Europe and on reflection is not deemed to signpost a structure for a Europe of the twenty-first century, then we simply have to go back to the drawing board.

I sincerely hope that at the end of the Intergovernmental Conference the British Government feels that this Constitution is good for Britain and good for Europe and that MPs and their constituents will be able to endorse it with enthusiasm. At the end of what is bound to be a tough Intergovernmental Conference I would like to be able to campaign alongside the Prime Minister for a yes vote both in Parliament and, if it were to come to it, in a referendum. However there is a lot of work to be done before that desirable outcome is achieved. And if the British Government feels, at the end of the Intergovernmental Conference, that the deal is bad for Britain and bad for Europe, then it should say so.

If a country, or several countries, fail to endorse the new Constitution, whether in a referendum or in their parliaments, the European Union will not collapse in a heap – the previous treaties still remain in place and the accession of new countries still goes ahead. Across the Union there are supporters and opponents of the treaty and all views should be heard. But most of those opposed to the Constitution are not saying 'scrap the European Union'. They are simply telling the politicians to come up with a political structure that ensures that, whatever level decisions are taken, the process is open and above board, and that those making them can be held to account. In other words a structure that is more in tune with the aspirations of Europe's peoples and less designed to meet the inclinations and ambitions of its bureaucrats and politicians.

Glossary

Acquis Communautaire The entire body of laws, policies and practices of the EU including not only the decisions of the Council of Ministers and the Commission but also all the rulings of the European Court of Justice.

Community method Describes the way the Union exercises its powers called competences. Essentially the Commission puts forward proposals and the Council of Ministers and the European Parliament make amendments. This right of co-decision will now be the rule with few exceptions in the area of Justice and Home Affairs and Common Foreign and Security Policy

Enhanced Cooperation Article 43 Countries can work together but only in those areas where the Union does not have exclusive competence and once it has been established that it cannot be done by all member states of the Union.

Passerelle Clause Article 24 [4] Areas which currently require unanimity could move to Qualified Majority Voting provided all members of the Council agree to this. The Council would have to consult with the European Parliament, but would no longer need the approval of all national parliaments.

Qualified Majority Voting Article 24 The Constitution proposes new weightings for Qualified Majority Voting (QMV) so that EU laws can be passed if half the members, representing at least 60 per cent of the population, vote for it. This will increase the weight of the larger states – Germany, France, Britain, Italy, Spain and Poland.

Structured Cooperation Article 40 [6] This only applies to the Common Security and Defence Policy. It allows a small group of countries to work together. Other countries will only be able to join later if the original group agrees.

Subsidiarity and Proportionality [Article 9 and Protocol attached to Treaty] Subsidiarity is the principle that decisions within the EU should be taken at the most local level feasible. Only decisions which can only be effective at supranational level should be taken at EU level. Proportionality means that Union action shall not go beyond what is necessary to achieve the objective.

The veto National vetoes will be abolished in at least 36 separate policy areas to avoid decision-making becoming paralysed in a Union of 25 members. Nevertheless, unanimity will remain for sensitive areas such as defence, foreign policy, tax and social security matters.